YOU'RE KIDDING...
I'M A SENIOR?

YOU'RE KIDDING...
I'M A SENIOR?

Renee' Servello

ReadersMagnet, LLC

You're Kidding...I'm A Senior?
Copyright © 2022 by Renee' Servello

Published in the United States of America
ISBN Paperback: 978-1-957312-33-0
ISBN Hardback: 978-1-957312-34-7
ISBN eBook: 978-1-957312-35-4

All rights reserved. No part of this publication may be reproduced, stored in a retrieval system or transmitted in any way by any means, electronic, mechanical, photocopy, recording or otherwise without the prior permission of the author except as provided by USA copyright law.

The opinions expressed by the author are not necessarily those of ReadersMagnet, LLC.

ReadersMagnet, LLC
10620 Treena Street, Suite 230 | San Diego, California, 92131 USA
1.619.354.2643 | www.readersmagnet.com

Book design copyright © 2022 by ReadersMagnet, LLC. All rights reserved.
Cover design by Kent Gabutin
Interior design by Don Anderson
Illustrations design by Michael Gillespie

For my wonderful husband, Anthony,
and our children, Kelli and Ty

For my hilarious mom, Joanne

It will be a good day! I will wake up, throw my feet on the floor, and hope ***LIFTOFF*** is successful!

Caffeine after 3:00 p.m. now equals an all-nighter.

When you wake up in the morning and *NOTHING* hurts, call 911...are you *ALIVE*?

Have you noticed that as your hair thins, your chin begins to look like a blooming *CHIA PET*?

Hair Loss

Have you noticed that as we age, our hair falls out more frequently? Yet, try plucking a hair out of your chin—you will find it embedded like cement!

Have you ever gone on a vacation and run across brochures of activities that are offered? Listed: zip-lining, white-water rafting, mountain climbing, horseback riding, skiing, mountain biking…

Then it hits you, ***WHAT AM I DOING HERE?***

Time changes…*REALLY?*

Fall back; spring forward. Going from Texas to California requires setting your watch back two hours. Now throw in the old "fall backward" one hour, and you have a very confused ***SENIOR***!

HAPPY HOUR was invented for ***SENIORS***…it ties right into the ***SUNSET DINNERS***.

Have you noticed that upon awakening, you now walk like a ***PENGUIN*** for the first two minutes of the day?

Where have all my eyelashes gone? Yes, folks, they ***FLUTTER*** away like the fall leaves.

Cardio classes can be equal to ***INSTANT DEATH***. ***NEVER*** watch the clock. The one-hour class will quickly seem like twelve hours!

SENIOR Sleeping

*It resembles the **WALTZ OF THE FLOWERS**, with constant movement from bed to couch, couch to recliner, and recliner back to bed. Folks, **SENIORS** are **BUSY!***

—Phil McCann

The Golden Years

There's no way you'll get through them without with a vat of Bengay and a heating pad!

Has everyone realized that pain moves? When you wake up in the morning, it's a crapshoot. It could be ***LURKING ANYWHERE***!

How come when your spouse forgets a word and you can't remember it either, he or she then blames *YOU*?

*When you stand suddenly after sitting for a while, remember to push the **PAUSE BUTTON**. You could end up flat on your back before the blood begins flowing!*

—*Phil McCann*

Sometimes we are asked in cardio class if we need a water break... **REALLY**? How about an oxygen break instead?

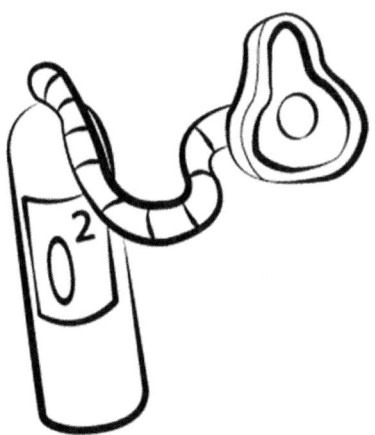

In my younger years, I used to think that if our house was ever broken into, I would just crawl out a window and ***RUN***! Now I can't even ***OPEN*** a window! Forget it—I'm all yours.

Hearing

These are the years when you tend to speak more softly. Why do family and friends then **YELL** at you? They obviously have a problem themselves, even though you are the one going **DEAF**!

I have long been aware of creases in clothing, paper, and so on. ***OMG***...I wasn't expecting my ***BODY*** to be creased!

Cars

Joy is a new car, and with that comes new dashboard symbols (Greek to me). Ultimate joy is getting the grandkids over *ASAP* to figure it all out for you.

Has anyone noticed the **_SHRINKING EFFECT_** as you age?

Just so you know…I am now a **_MUSHROOM_**!

What does it say about your friends, when everyone pulls out flip phones? It says, **NO ONE** in **THIS** group is worried about phones being stolen!

Yard Work

SENIORS must first convince the knees to bend. Who will pick you up later? ***BAD IDEA, FOLKS!***

Making Lists

More important than a birth certificate.
SENIORS CANNOT MOVE or shouldn't without one!
Guaranteed to keep you on track and focused.

Let's talk *VEINS*. Why, oh why, do I now look like *SPIDER-MAN*?

How many times have you opened your mouth to swallow a pill, taken a drink of water, and then **SURPRISE**...discovered the pill on the floor the next day?

Folks, do you suffer from ***MARSHMALLOW FACE*** in the a.m.? (This is also known as puffiness.) Don't panic…just remember that fluid drains!

Wrinkles are free; they can't be ordered off the Internet.

—Susie Sellier

A World of Whisperers

You know it's true; everyone ***WHISPERS*** now. Luckily, I am still sharing my gift of a loud voice with the world. However, it seems like ***NO ONE RECIPROCATES…*** they continue to ***WHISPER***.

Communication

My husband and I sometimes visit the same doctor. When we leave the office, my husband remembers the doctor's instructions one way, and my memory is the total opposite of his. I guess our communication and hearing skills just took a ***LONG HIKE***!

You visit your ear doctor, expecting to be told that it might be time for hearing aids. Instead, you hear the word **_WAX_** and are deliriously happy!

You again visit the ear doctor and are told, "No, it is not *WAX*. You are *DEAF*!"

You know you are older when you wake up and have to look at your pill container box to know what day of the week it is.

—*Phil McCann*

I love the smell of Salonpas in the morning!

—*Gail Bloomer*

If you have a vegan houseguest, remember what that actually means for *YOU*…days of chopping veggies! That could *KILL* a *SENIOR*!

A grandchild is a true blessing. So why are we **WORN OUT** after this blessing has visited for only a few hours?

Pluck, Pluck

During your teenage years, you pluck your eyebrows.

After fifty, you pluck your chin.

After sixty, you pluck your neck and ears.

After that…let's not go there!

The more you learn, the more you earn.

—Susie Sellier

Mission Impossible

You girls know what I'm talking about: Spanx or similar concealing garments. You'll need two girlfriends standing by to help with the "try-on" project. Mama never said life would be easy!

It doesn't take a team; it takes the Internet

—*Judy Kirk*

Arms

What a shock! Raise your arm to wave at someone, and you may be smacked in the face…*DUCK*! It's the dreaded *ARM FLAB,* folks.

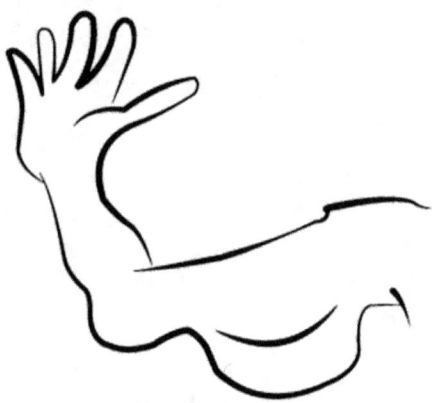

White-Coat Syndrome

It is spreading like wildfire. Your blood pressure shoots up to unimaginable heights when visiting your doctor. **OMG**, *what to do? Rather than take a pulse, laugh out loud so that your doctor will know an ambulance is not necessary!*

—Dallas Peterson

Exercise

After one hour of this fun, we go home and pass out. Who said this stuff ***REVITALIZES*** you? I didn't get that memo.

Are we traveling too often? I reached into the closet to grab a suitcase, and it screamed, "*NO, LEAVE ME ALONE!*" Luggage now talks back, folks.

Happiness is a TV remote that actually says *MUTE* versus another stupid symbol!

When a **_SENIOR_** says he or she is booked solid for a week…that's code for a million doctor's appointments!

Happiness is looking forward, not backward.

Who out there thinks the dining room table is for dining? Let's be honest…it has stacks and stacks of VIS (very important stuff) on it. You can forget about meals!

SENIOR Math

One cup of coffee in the a.m. equals eighteen trips to the restroom in the next hour!

Have you realized that you could stuff a pillow with your current hair loss? ***THAT'S JUST SAD!***

Long-Term Life Insurance

If you sign up for it, be prepared for tough questions. My first question was "What day of the week is it?" Talk about feeling like a total ***FAILURE*** when I got ***THAT*** wrong!

*Sometimes you have so much to do that you get agitated. Sit down, do nothing, reflect, and **THEN** you all of sudden feel **PRODUCTIVE**!*

—Joanne Cotten

Staying Healthy/Exercise

You go into rooms repeatedly, forget why, and retrace your steps. It's called ***RECALCULATING***, folks. You try this several times, and guess what? That is your new ***EXERCISE PROGRAM***!

Why do some **_SENIORS_** scream into a phone like they are talking to someone in Afghanistan?

Some of us are known for wishing others a "good weekend" when actually it is only Monday. Yes, sometimes keeping up with the days of the week can become ***MISSION IMPOSSIBLE***! It's a good line to really confuse people, ***PLUS*** yourself!

Restaurants are now chosen by noise level. ***OMG***…is it time to just throw in the towel and stay home to ***COOK***? ***HORRORS!***

Wealth of Problems

On your bedside table, you may possibly have the following:

1. A remote for your Number Bed
2. A talking remote for your TV
3. Possibly another remote for the TV
4. A telephone
5. A cell phone

Quick, call Mark Burnett—this has the makings of a TV sitcom!

Isn't it fun to update your phone? A thousand pages of instructions later and you *MAY* catch on!

Note to Engineers

SENIORS are the on/off generation. Going through twelve prompts to turn on a TV is highly overrated.

Dry Cleaning Miracle

If you have heated seats in your car, then you are set! Turn on the heat, ride around for a while, and jump out. Then you are **READY**! You have arrived with perfect seams in your slacks. Clever **SENIORS**!

OK, folks, there's just nothing like having new TV boxes installed. After considerable time spent turning them on with no picture…do what you must. We called the troops over…our seven-year-old grandson. Yes, we are ***PATHETIC***!

*Are you spotted yet? Well, it's coming. Little white spots all over your skin. Just pretend it's snowing, and hope it doesn't reach **BLIZZARD** stage!*

—Anthony Servello

*When a **SENIOR** bends over to pick up something, that's **NOT** amazing. What's amazing is if he or she is able to **GET UP AGAIN!***

—Jo Fuchs

Death by Travel

My husband loves to travel. His reasoning is that we must go while the body will go. So, if I'm fatigued *NOW*, then the next step must be ***DEATH***. My question is… what happened to the in-between stage?

Body Wrinkles

Time for pool and spa coverings! We simply don't need more sun, which translates to *MORE WRINKLES*. Have you ever seen a prune?

When, oh when, can I have that very important alone time? Translated: I must try new eye creams that ***SWEAR*** I will never have puffy eyes again. Of course I believe all the advertising!

Pill Poppers

You will recognize this drill. You go out to eat with friends. Upon being seated, the first thing everyone requests is a glass of water from the waiter. Within seconds, all pill containers are on the table, ***UNLOCKED AND LOADED.*** You guessed it—time for ***EVERYONE*** to take a pill!

SENIORS Dining Out

A group of SENIORS dining out...the waitstaff should expect a minimum of five questions per person if they are lucky. *SENIORS* are an inquisitive bunch!

SENIORS might consider skipping buffets. Your eyes say *YES*; meanwhile, the stomach is readying for the *REVOLT*!

Eyes

Did you realize when you went from the well-rested look to the **_RING-AROUND-THE-EYES_** look? Don't panic. Not only have you aged, you now have **_RACCOON EYES_**!

Have you noticed that your ears play tricks on you sometimes? A person can be speaking to you, and there may be a word that you just don't understand. You finally yell, "***SPELL IT.***" Is this conversation ever going to end, and do you now have ***MUSH EARS***? ***OMG***!

Post-It Notes

Everyone knows Post-It Notes were invented by scientists from the 3M company. Hold on, folks…I began cutting squares of papers and hanging them all over our apartment in my early twenties. What this tells us is that there is **NO** hope for me. I sincerely hope **YOUR** memory is better than mine!

Remember, folks…we all have an expiration date, so make the most of your ***SHELF LIFE***!

Girls, I pray to God that when *MY* shelf life expires, I am in ***FULL MAKEUP***!

*This should ring a bell with all **SENIORS**. You call tech support for your computer, and you immediately throw the phone over to your son or daughter when the company responds. The reason you do this is because you automatically know it will all sound like a foreign language. For some reason, the son or daughter does not look at you with love once they have ended **YOUR** call with tech support. Just give up, and invite the kid to dinner.*

—Ty Servello

Tattooed by Nature

*Grandchildren seem to look at SENIORS with admiration when they think they might have **TATs**. Then then realize they are clumps of blue veins. No surprise—you are no longer **HOT STUFF**!*

—Dallas Peterson

SKIN TAGS

You wake up one day, look in the mirror, and scream.

Little globs of skin all over your face and body. Is it my diet or medications? ***OMG***! Give me a ***LASER, ASAP***!

Lazy Lips

Have you noticed some people just don't open their lips when speaking? What comes out of their mouths is all garbled. Honestly, folks, ***STOP MAKING MY LIFE MORE CHALLENGING!***

Opening Jars

Another *MISSION IMPOSSIBLE* for *SENIORS*. Memo to manufacturers: just include a can of WD-40!

SENIOR Heat Treatment

Get in a car with heated seats. Turn those suckers **_ON_**. Drive around for a while with the heat on, depending on the pain level. Exit the car. You are now **_NEW AND IMPROVED_** and have your car to thank for feeling so good. Absolutely brilliant!

Pluck, Pluck

Have you noticed that when you pluck a hair out of your eyebrow, skin now comes with it? That's because your upper eyelid is now *LOOSE*, fondly known as *DROOPY LIDS*!

Magnifying Mirrors

Do away with them ASAP. Do you really need to see ***DESTRUCTION UP CLOSE***?

More Veins

You are propped up in bed, legs thrown out in front of you. You see more blue veins on the legs, ankles, and feet. You know what that means! You have now become ***BLUE SPIDER-MAN***!

Folks, I *KNOW* I could be thin. I just need to be ***STRETCHED***. So what's the problem?

SENIORS slicing their own bagels could mean "losing-a-finger day." That will translate to blood, hospital, and stitches. Do you ***REALLY*** want that bagel?

Your sixteen-year-old granddaughter enters your closet and spies the row of black slacks. "How many black slacks do you really need?" she asks.

The simple answer is: "As many as I can cram in here!" Let's all remember what black does for the figure.

Save Those Eyeballs

I'm taking a sabbatical from technology today before my eyes fall out. Like, who would put them back in?

—*Susie Sellier*

If you miss three weeks of your cardio class, here's a hint. Have an ambulance standing by for your ***RE-ENTRY DAY***!

Building Character

*You know this is familiar. Your kids drop by, and you pull out **THE LIST**. "Do you have time to change a light bulb, make changes to the computer, change cartridges in the printer, find the lost phone numbers on the iPhone, dig up a tree or bush, unstop the shower and toilet, get the car running, hang a picture, bathe the dog, cook dinner on the grill?"*

"You do? Great! Now when is your next visit?"

—Anthony Servello

Have a fluffy bed with pillows and more pillows? If so, you need to make a major decision. Make the bed completely every day, or…be a ***SENIOR***, and say enough is enough. Easy answer, folks!

When climbing into the rear seat of a passenger van, your ***BACKSIDE*** will be highly visible. Think about that for a minute!

Multitasking

Who are we kidding here? *IF* we accomplish one task a day, *THAT* is known as a ***SENIOR MIRACLE***.

Trouble is lurking *EVERYWHERE*! Miss a chair, and it could be *LIGHTS OUT*!

Dear TSA and other security personnel in airports:

When you see a **_SENIOR_**, please no shouting or giving instructions in machine-gun delivery. Remember that **_SENIORS_** have a hard time bending over to remove **_ANYTHING_**. Our hearing, bodies, and understanding only operate on **_SLOW._**

Think of yourself as a flower. It's never too late to bloom like the spring flowers. Just keep on blooming, folks!

Acknowledgments

Anthony Servello
Ty Servello
Joanne Cotten
Dallas Peterson
Jo Fuchs
Susie Sellier
Phil McCain
Gail Bloomer
Carrie Russ Gimmestad and the Memorial Athletic Club

About the Author

The author's book is being published strictly for medicinal purposes…Laugh out loud, and you'll be fine.

Remember, we're all aging daily. Try to have a few laughs along the way.

You can reach the author at: reneeservello@att.net.

www.ingramcontent.com/pod-product-compliance
Lightning Source LLC
LaVergne TN
LVHW020424080526
838202LV00055B/5023